Savor the Spuds

Creative Potato Tray with Chicken Recipes

While every precaution has been taken in the preparation of this book, the publisher assumes no responsibility for errors or omissions, or for damages resulting from the use of the information contained herein.

SAVOR THE SPUDS

First edition. March 11, 2024.

ISBN: 979-8224791293

Written by Jose Maria.

Table of Contents

Jose Maria

❖ Introduction to Potato Tray with Chicken Cooking

Potatoes and chicken are two staple ingredients in many cuisines around the world. Their versatility makes them perfect companions in a wide range of dishes, from comforting classics to innovative creations. When combined and cooked together on a tray, they create a hearty and satisfying meal that is easy to prepare and loved by many.

A. The Versatility of Potatoes and Chicken

Potatoes are incredibly versatile tubers that can be prepared in numerous ways, including boiling, baking, frying, and roasting. They can be sliced, diced, mashed, or left whole, offering endless possibilities for creating diverse dishes.

Chicken, on the other hand, is a versatile protein that can be cooked in various methods such as grilling, baking, frying, or stewing. It pairs well with a wide range of flavors and ingredients, making it a favorite choice for many dishes worldwide.

Combining potatoes and chicken not only adds flavor and texture contrast to a dish but also ensures a well-balanced meal with carbohydrates, proteins, and essential nutrients.

B. Advantages of Using a Tray for Cooking

Using a tray for cooking potatoes and chicken offers several advantages:

1. Even Cooking: A tray provides a large surface area, allowing for even distribution of heat, resulting in evenly cooked potatoes and chicken.
2. Convenience: Cooking everything on one tray simplifies the cooking process and reduces cleanup time.
3. Flavor Infusion: When potatoes and chicken are cooked

together on a tray, their flavors meld together, creating a deliciously cohesive dish.

4. Versatility: A tray allows for easy customization by adding various herbs, spices, and vegetables to create different flavor profiles.

C. Tips for Selecting the Best Potatoes and Chicken Cuts

1. Potatoes: Choose potatoes that are firm, smooth-skinned, and free of blemishes. Different varieties, such as russet, Yukon Gold, or red potatoes, offer varying textures and flavors, so select the type that best suits your recipe.

2. Chicken Cuts: When selecting chicken cuts for tray cooking, consider the cooking time and desired texture. Bone-in, skin-on cuts, such as chicken thighs or drumsticks, are ideal for longer cooking times, as they remain juicy and flavorful. Boneless, skinless chicken breasts cook faster and are well-suited for recipes that require shorter cooking times.

By following these tips and utilizing the versatility of potatoes and chicken, you can create delicious and satisfying meals that are sure to please your family and friends. Let's move on to the essential techniques and tips for preparing a potato tray with chicken.

Chapter (1) Essential Techniques and Tips

A. Preparing the Tray for Cooking

1. Choose the Right Tray: Select a sturdy, rimmed baking tray or sheet pan that can accommodate both the chicken and potatoes without overcrowding. A non-stick surface or lining the tray with parchment paper can help prevent sticking.
2. Grease the Tray: Lightly grease the tray with cooking spray, olive oil, or butter to prevent sticking and facilitate easy cleanup.
3. Arrange Ingredients: Arrange the chicken and potatoes in a single layer on the tray, ensuring that there is some space between each piece to allow for even cooking. Avoid overcrowding the tray, as this can lead to uneven cooking and steaming instead of roasting.
4. Preheat the Oven: Preheat your oven to the recommended temperature specified in your recipe. A preheated oven ensures that the chicken and potatoes start cooking immediately, promoting browning and caramelization.

B. Seasoning and Marinating Chicken

1. Seasoning: Season the chicken generously with salt and pepper, as well as any additional herbs, spices, or seasoning blends according to your preference or recipe. Ensure that both sides of the chicken are evenly seasoned for maximum flavor.
2. Marinating: Marinating the chicken adds depth of flavor and helps tenderize the meat. Prepare a marinade using ingredients such as olive oil, lemon juice, garlic, herbs, and spices. Place the chicken in a resealable plastic bag or shallow dish, pour the marinade over it, and refrigerate for at least 30 minutes or up to

overnight for optimal flavor.

3. Brining (Optional): For extra juicy and flavorful chicken, consider brining the chicken before cooking. To brine, dissolve salt and sugar in water, immerse the chicken in the brine, and refrigerate for a few hours before cooking.

C. Potato Preparation Techniques (Slicing, Dicing, etc.)

1. Slicing: For classic roasted potatoes, slice them into even-sized rounds or wedges. Ensure uniform thickness to promote even cooking.
2. Dicing: Dicing potatoes into cubes is ideal for dishes like chicken and potato hash or casseroles. Aim for uniformity in size to ensure even cooking.
3. Leaving Whole: Leaving smaller potatoes whole, especially baby potatoes or new potatoes, is a simple yet delicious option. Simply wash and scrub them before cooking.
4. Parboiling (Optional): If you prefer softer potatoes with a creamy interior, consider parboiling them before adding to the tray. Boil the potatoes for a few minutes until slightly tender, then drain and pat dry before seasoning and roasting.

D. Proper Temperature and Timing for Cooking

1. Temperature: Roast the chicken and potatoes in a preheated oven at a temperature between 375°F to 425°F (190°C to 220°C), depending on the recipe. Higher temperatures promote browning and crispiness, while lower temperatures ensure a more gentle cooking process.
2. Timing: The cooking time will vary depending on the size and thickness of the chicken pieces and potatoes. Generally, chicken thighs and drumsticks require 35-45 minutes, while chicken breasts may need 25-35 minutes. Potatoes typically take 30-45

minutes to roast, depending on their size and preparation method. Use a meat thermometer to ensure the chicken reaches an internal temperature of 165°F (74°C) for safety.

By following these essential techniques and tips, you'll be well-equipped to prepare a delicious potato tray with chicken that's perfectly seasoned, cooked, and ready to enjoy. Let me know if you'd like to move on to one of the recipes from the outline!

Chapter (2) Classic Potato Tray with Chicken Recipes

A. Traditional Roasted Chicken and Potato Tray
Ingredients:

- 4 bone-in, skin-on chicken thighs
- 4 medium russet potatoes, washed and cut into wedges
- 2 tablespoons olive oil
- 2 cloves garlic, minced
- 1 teaspoon dried thyme
- 1 teaspoon dried rosemary
- Salt and black pepper to taste
- Fresh parsley, chopped (for garnish)

Instructions:

1. Preheat your oven to 400°F (200°C). Grease a baking tray with cooking spray or olive oil.
2. In a small bowl, mix together olive oil, minced garlic, dried thyme, dried rosemary, salt, and black pepper.
3. Place the chicken thighs and potato wedges on the prepared baking tray.
4. Brush the olive oil mixture over the chicken thighs and potato wedges, ensuring they are evenly coated.
5. Roast in the preheated oven for 35-40 minutes, or until the chicken is cooked through and the potatoes are golden brown and crispy.
6. Garnish with chopped fresh parsley before serving. Enjoy your traditional roasted chicken and potato tray!

- Note: Make sure to check the internal temperature of the

chicken thighs, which should reach 165°F (74°C) to ensure they are fully cooked.

B. Lemon Herb Chicken with Garlic Roasted Potatoes
Ingredients:
For the Chicken:

- 4 boneless, skinless chicken breasts
- Zest of 1 lemon
- Juice of 1 lemon
- 2 cloves garlic, minced
- 2 tablespoons olive oil
- 1 teaspoon dried thyme
- 1 teaspoon dried rosemary
- Salt and black pepper to taste

For the Potatoes:

- 4 medium Yukon Gold potatoes, washed and cut into 1-inch cubes
- 3 tablespoons olive oil
- 3 cloves garlic, minced
- 1 teaspoon dried thyme
- 1 teaspoon dried rosemary
- Salt and black pepper to taste
- Fresh parsley, chopped (for garnish)

Instructions:

1. Preheat your oven to 400°F (200°C). Grease a baking tray with cooking spray or olive oil.
2. In a small bowl, prepare the marinade for the chicken by mixing together the lemon zest, lemon juice, minced garlic, olive oil, dried thyme, dried rosemary, salt, and black pepper.

3. Place the chicken breasts in a resealable plastic bag or shallow dish and pour the marinade over them, ensuring they are evenly coated. Marinate in the refrigerator for at least 30 minutes, or up to 4 hours for maximum flavor.

4. In another bowl, toss the cubed potatoes with olive oil, minced garlic, dried thyme, dried rosemary, salt, and black pepper until well coated.

5. Arrange the marinated chicken breasts and seasoned potatoes on the prepared baking tray, ensuring they are in a single layer and not overcrowded.

6. Roast in the preheated oven for 25-30 minutes, or until the chicken is cooked through (internal temperature of 165°F/ 74°C) and the potatoes are golden brown and crispy, stirring the potatoes halfway through cooking.

7. Once cooked, remove from the oven and let the chicken rest for a few minutes before serving.

8. Garnish with chopped fresh parsley before serving. Enjoy your lemon herb chicken with garlic roasted potatoes!

C. Paprika-Spiced Chicken and Potato Tray
Ingredients:
For the Chicken:

- 4 bone-in, skin-on chicken drumsticks
- 2 tablespoons olive oil
- 2 teaspoons smoked paprika
- 1 teaspoon garlic powder
- 1 teaspoon onion powder
- 1 teaspoon dried oregano
- 1 teaspoon dried thyme
- Salt and black pepper to taste

For the Potatoes:

- 4 medium red potatoes, washed and cut into wedges
- 2 tablespoons olive oil
- 1 teaspoon smoked paprika
- 1 teaspoon garlic powder
- Salt and black pepper to taste
- Fresh parsley, chopped (for garnish)

Instructions:

1. Preheat your oven to 400°F (200°C). Grease a baking tray with cooking spray or olive oil.
2. In a small bowl, prepare the marinade for the chicken by mixing together olive oil, smoked paprika, garlic powder, onion powder, dried oregano, dried thyme, salt, and black pepper.
3. Place the chicken drumsticks in a resealable plastic bag or shallow dish and pour the marinade over them, ensuring they are evenly coated. Marinate in the refrigerator for at least 30 minutes.
4. In another bowl, toss the potato wedges with olive oil, smoked paprika, garlic powder, salt, and black pepper until well coated.
5. Arrange the marinated chicken drumsticks and seasoned potato wedges on the prepared baking tray, ensuring they are in a single layer.
6. Roast in the preheated oven for 35-40 minutes, or until the chicken is cooked through (internal temperature of 165°F/ 74°C) and the potatoes are golden brown and crispy, flipping the potatoes halfway through cooking.
7. Once cooked, remove from the oven and let the chicken rest for a few minutes before serving.
8. Garnish with chopped fresh parsley before serving. Enjoy your paprika-spiced chicken and potato tray!

D. Italian-inspired Chicken Parmesan with Potato Wedges
Ingredients:
For the Chicken Parmesan:

- 4 boneless, skinless chicken breasts
- Salt and black pepper to taste
- 1 cup all-purpose flour
- 2 large eggs, beaten
- 1 cup breadcrumbs (preferably seasoned)
- 1 cup marinara sauce
- 1 cup shredded mozzarella cheese
- 1/4 cup grated Parmesan cheese
- Fresh basil leaves, chopped (for garnish)

For the Potato Wedges:

- 4 medium russet potatoes, washed and cut into wedges
- 2 tablespoons olive oil
- 1 teaspoon dried oregano
- 1 teaspoon dried basil
- 1 teaspoon garlic powder
- Salt and black pepper to taste

Instructions:

1. Preheat your oven to 400°F (200°C). Grease a baking tray with cooking spray or olive oil.
2. Season the chicken breasts with salt and black pepper to taste.
3. Set up three shallow bowls for dredging the chicken: one with flour, one with beaten eggs, and one with breadcrumbs.
4. Dredge each chicken breast in the flour, shaking off any excess, then dip it into the beaten eggs, and finally coat it with

breadcrumbs, pressing gently to adhere.

5. Place the breaded chicken breasts on one side of the prepared baking tray.

6. In a separate bowl, toss the potato wedges with olive oil, dried oregano, dried basil, garlic powder, salt, and black pepper until well coated.

7. Arrange the seasoned potato wedges on the other side of the baking tray, ensuring they are in a single layer and not overcrowded.

8. Bake in the preheated oven for 20 minutes.

9. After 20 minutes, remove the tray from the oven and spoon marinara sauce over each chicken breast. Sprinkle shredded mozzarella cheese and grated Parmesan cheese over the sauce.

10. Return the tray to the oven and bake for an additional 15-20 minutes, or until the chicken is cooked through (internal temperature of 165°F/74°C), the cheese is melted and bubbly, and the potato wedges are golden brown and crispy.

11. Once cooked, remove from the oven and let the chicken rest for a few minutes before serving.

12. Garnish with chopped fresh basil leaves before serving. Enjoy your Italian-inspired chicken Parmesan with potato wedges!

E. Barbecue Chicken Drumsticks with Sweet Potato Fries
Ingredients:
For the Barbecue Chicken Drumsticks:

- 8 chicken drumsticks
- 1 cup barbecue sauce (homemade or store-bought)
- 2 tablespoons olive oil
- 1 tablespoon soy sauce
- 1 tablespoon Worcestershire sauce
- 1 teaspoon garlic powder
- Salt and black pepper to taste

- Fresh cilantro or parsley, chopped (for garnish)

For the Sweet Potato Fries:

- 2 large sweet potatoes, peeled and cut into fries
- 2 tablespoons olive oil
- 1 teaspoon paprika
- 1 teaspoon garlic powder
- Salt and black pepper to taste

Instructions:

1. Preheat your oven to 425°F (220°C). Grease a baking tray with cooking spray or olive oil.
2. In a bowl, whisk together barbecue sauce, olive oil, soy sauce, Worcestershire sauce, garlic powder, salt, and black pepper to create the marinade for the chicken drumsticks.
3. Place the chicken drumsticks in a large resealable plastic bag or shallow dish. Pour the marinade over the chicken, ensuring it's evenly coated. Marinate in the refrigerator for at least 30 minutes, or up to 4 hours for maximum flavor.
4. In another bowl, toss the sweet potato fries with olive oil, paprika, garlic powder, salt, and black pepper until well coated.
5. Arrange the marinated chicken drumsticks and sweet potato fries on the prepared baking tray, ensuring they are in a single layer.
6. Bake in the preheated oven for 35-40 minutes, or until the chicken is cooked through (internal temperature of 165°F/ 74°C), and the sweet potato fries are golden brown and crispy, flipping the fries halfway through cooking.
7. Once cooked, remove from the oven and let the chicken rest for a few minutes before serving.
8. Garnish the barbecue chicken drumsticks with chopped fresh

cilantro or parsley before serving. Enjoy your delicious barbecue chicken drumsticks with sweet potato fries!

Chapter (3) Creative Twists on Potato Tray with Chicken

A. Mediterranean Chicken and Potato Bake with Olives and Feta

Ingredients:

For the Chicken:

- 4 bone-in, skin-on chicken thighs
- 2 tablespoons olive oil
- 2 cloves garlic, minced
- 1 teaspoon dried oregano
- 1 teaspoon dried basil
- Salt and black pepper to taste

For the Potatoes:

- 4 medium red potatoes, washed and cut into wedges
- 2 tablespoons olive oil
- 1 teaspoon dried oregano
- 1 teaspoon dried thyme
- Salt and black pepper to taste

Additional Ingredients:

- 1/2 cup Kalamata olives, pitted
- 1/2 cup crumbled feta cheese
- Fresh parsley, chopped (for garnish)

Instructions:

1. Preheat your oven to 400°F (200°C). Grease a baking tray with cooking spray or olive oil.

2. In a small bowl, prepare the marinade for the chicken by mixing together olive oil, minced garlic, dried oregano, dried basil, salt, and black pepper.
3. Place the chicken thighs in a resealable plastic bag or shallow dish and pour the marinade over them, ensuring they are evenly coated. Marinate in the refrigerator for at least 30 minutes.
4. In another bowl, toss the potato wedges with olive oil, dried oregano, dried thyme, salt, and black pepper until well coated.
5. Arrange the marinated chicken thighs and seasoned potato wedges on the prepared baking tray, ensuring they are in a single layer.
6. Scatter Kalamata olives over the chicken and potatoes.
7. Bake in the preheated oven for 35-40 minutes, or until the chicken is cooked through (internal temperature of 165°F/ 74°C) and the potatoes are golden brown and crispy.
8. Sprinkle crumbled feta cheese over the chicken and potatoes during the last 5 minutes of baking.
9. Once cooked, remove from the oven and let the chicken rest for a few minutes before serving.
10. Garnish with chopped fresh parsley before serving. Enjoy your Mediterranean chicken and potato bake with olives and feta!

B. Thai Coconut Curry Chicken with Roasted Potatoes
Ingredients:
For the Chicken:

- 4 boneless, skinless chicken breasts, sliced into strips
- 2 tablespoons vegetable oil
- 3 tablespoons Thai red curry paste
- 1 can (13.5 oz) coconut milk
- 2 tablespoons fish sauce
- 1 tablespoon brown sugar
- 1 red bell pepper, thinly sliced

- 1 small onion, thinly sliced
- 2 cloves garlic, minced
- Salt and pepper to taste
- Fresh cilantro leaves, chopped (for garnish)
- Lime wedges (for serving)

For the Potatoes:

- 4 medium sweet potatoes, peeled and cut into chunks
- 2 tablespoons vegetable oil
- 1 teaspoon ground turmeric
- 1 teaspoon ground cumin
- Salt and pepper to taste

Instructions:

1. Preheat your oven to 425°F (220°C). Grease a baking tray with cooking spray or vegetable oil.
2. In a bowl, toss the sweet potato chunks with vegetable oil, ground turmeric, ground cumin, salt, and pepper until evenly coated. Spread them out in a single layer on the prepared baking tray.
3. Roast the sweet potatoes in the preheated oven for 25-30 minutes, or until tender and lightly browned, stirring halfway through cooking.
4. While the sweet potatoes are roasting, heat the vegetable oil in a large skillet over medium heat. Add the sliced chicken breasts and cook until browned on all sides, about 5-6 minutes.
5. Add the Thai red curry paste to the skillet and stir to coat the chicken evenly.
6. Pour in the coconut milk, fish sauce, and brown sugar. Stir to combine and bring to a simmer.
7. Add the sliced red bell pepper, onion, and minced garlic to

the skillet. Stir well and continue to simmer for another 5-7 minutes, or until the vegetables are tender and the chicken is cooked through.

8. Season the coconut curry chicken with salt and pepper to taste.
9. Serve the Thai coconut curry chicken alongside the roasted sweet potatoes.
10. Garnish with chopped cilantro leaves and serve with lime wedges on the side for squeezing over the chicken. Enjoy your delicious Thai coconut curry chicken with roasted potatoes!

C. Mexican-inspired Chicken Fajita Potato Tray
Ingredients:
For the Chicken Fajitas:

- 4 boneless, skinless chicken breasts, thinly sliced
- 2 tablespoons olive oil
- 1 tablespoon chili powder
- 1 teaspoon ground cumin
- 1 teaspoon smoked paprika
- 1 teaspoon garlic powder
- 1 teaspoon onion powder
- Salt and black pepper to taste
- Juice of 1 lime
- 1 red bell pepper, thinly sliced
- 1 green bell pepper, thinly sliced
- 1 onion, thinly sliced

For the Potatoes:

- 4 medium russet potatoes, washed and cut into wedges
- 2 tablespoons olive oil
- 1 teaspoon chili powder

- 1 teaspoon smoked paprika
- Salt and black pepper to taste

For Serving:

- Warm tortillas
- Guacamole
- Sour cream
- Salsa
- Fresh cilantro, chopped

Instructions:

1. Preheat your oven to 425°F (220°C). Grease a baking tray with cooking spray or olive oil.
2. In a large bowl, toss the sliced chicken breasts with olive oil, chili powder, ground cumin, smoked paprika, garlic powder, onion powder, salt, black pepper, and lime juice until evenly coated. Set aside to marinate while you prepare the potatoes.
3. In another bowl, toss the potato wedges with olive oil, chili powder, smoked paprika, salt, and black pepper until well coated.
4. Arrange the marinated chicken slices, sliced bell peppers, and onion on one side of the prepared baking tray, ensuring they are in a single layer.
5. Place the seasoned potato wedges on the other side of the baking tray, ensuring they are in a single layer and not overcrowded.
6. Roast in the preheated oven for 25-30 minutes, or until the chicken is cooked through and the potatoes are golden brown and crispy, stirring the vegetables and flipping the potatoes halfway through cooking.
7. Once cooked, remove from the oven and let the chicken and

potatoes rest for a few minutes before serving.

8. Serve the Mexican-inspired chicken fajitas and roasted potatoes with warm tortillas, guacamole, sour cream, salsa, and chopped fresh cilantro for garnish.

9. Allow everyone to assemble their own fajitas with their desired toppings. Enjoy your flavorful Mexican-inspired chicken fajita potato tray!

D. Teriyaki Glazed Chicken Thighs with Sesame Roasted Potatoes

Ingredients:

For the Teriyaki Glazed Chicken Thighs:

- 8 bone-in, skin-on chicken thighs
- 1/2 cup soy sauce
- 1/4 cup brown sugar
- 2 cloves garlic, minced
- 1 tablespoon grated ginger
- 2 tablespoons rice vinegar
- 2 tablespoons mirin (Japanese sweet rice wine)
- 1 tablespoon sesame oil
- 2 tablespoons water
- 1 tablespoon cornstarch
- Sesame seeds, for garnish
- Sliced green onions, for garnish

For the Sesame Roasted Potatoes:

- 4 medium Yukon Gold potatoes, washed and cut into chunks
- 2 tablespoons olive oil
- 1 tablespoon soy sauce
- 1 tablespoon sesame oil
- 1 tablespoon sesame seeds

- Salt and black pepper to taste

Instructions:

1. Preheat your oven to 425°F (220°C). Grease a baking tray with cooking spray or olive oil.
2. In a small saucepan, combine soy sauce, brown sugar, minced garlic, grated ginger, rice vinegar, mirin, and sesame oil for the teriyaki glaze. Bring to a simmer over medium heat and cook for 2-3 minutes.
3. In a small bowl, mix together water and cornstarch to create a slurry. Slowly add the slurry to the saucepan, whisking continuously, until the sauce thickens. Remove from heat and set aside.
4. In a large bowl, toss the potato chunks with olive oil, soy sauce, sesame oil, sesame seeds, salt, and black pepper until well coated. Spread them out in a single layer on the prepared baking tray.
5. Place the chicken thighs on the baking tray, skin side up, next to the potatoes.
6. Brush the teriyaki glaze over the chicken thighs, ensuring they are evenly coated.
7. Roast in the preheated oven for 35-40 minutes, or until the chicken is cooked through (internal temperature of 165°F/ 74°C) and the potatoes are golden brown and crispy.
8. Once cooked, remove from the oven and let the chicken and potatoes rest for a few minutes before serving.
9. Garnish the teriyaki glazed chicken thighs with sesame seeds and sliced green onions before serving.
10. Serve the chicken thighs and sesame roasted potatoes hot, accompanied by steamed vegetables or a side salad. Enjoy your delicious teriyaki glazed chicken thighs with sesame roasted potatoes!

E. Indian Tandoori Chicken with Spiced Potato Medley

Ingredients:

For the Tandoori Chicken:

- 8 chicken drumsticks
- 1 cup plain yogurt
- 2 tablespoons lemon juice
- 2 tablespoons tandoori masala spice blend
- 1 tablespoon minced garlic
- 1 tablespoon minced ginger
- 1 teaspoon ground cumin
- 1 teaspoon ground coriander
- 1/2 teaspoon smoked paprika
- Salt to taste
- Fresh cilantro, chopped (for garnish)
- Lemon wedges, for serving

For the Spiced Potato Medley:

- 4 medium potatoes, washed and cut into chunks
- 2 tablespoons olive oil
- 1 teaspoon ground turmeric
- 1 teaspoon ground cumin
- 1 teaspoon ground coriander
- 1/2 teaspoon cayenne pepper (optional, for extra heat)
- Salt and black pepper to taste
- Fresh cilantro, chopped (for garnish)

Instructions:

1. In a large bowl, combine plain yogurt, lemon juice, tandoori masala spice blend, minced garlic, minced ginger, ground cumin, ground coriander, smoked paprika, and salt to taste. Mix well to form the marinade.

2. Add the chicken drumsticks to the marinade, ensuring they are evenly coated. Cover the bowl and marinate the chicken in the refrigerator for at least 2 hours, or preferably overnight, to allow the flavors to develop.

3. Preheat your oven to 425°F (220°C). Grease a baking tray with cooking spray or olive oil.

4. In a separate bowl, toss the potato chunks with olive oil, ground turmeric, ground cumin, ground coriander, cayenne pepper (if using), salt, and black pepper until well coated.

5. Spread the seasoned potato chunks out in a single layer on one side of the prepared baking tray.

6. Remove the chicken drumsticks from the marinade, shaking off any excess, and place them on the other side of the baking tray.

7. Roast in the preheated oven for 30-35 minutes, or until the chicken is cooked through (internal temperature of 165°F/ 74°C) and the potatoes are tender and golden brown, flipping the chicken halfway through cooking.

8. Once cooked, remove from the oven and let the chicken and potatoes rest for a few minutes before serving.

9. Garnish the tandoori chicken with chopped fresh cilantro and serve with lemon wedges on the side.

10. Serve the tandoori chicken with the spiced potato medley hot, accompanied by naan bread or rice, and your favorite chutneys or raita. Enjoy your flavorful Indian tandoori chicken with spiced potato medley!

Chapter (4) Vegetarian/Vegan Options

A. Herb-Roasted Potatoes with Baked Tofu Strips
  Ingredients:
  For the Herb-Roasted Potatoes:

- 4 medium potatoes, washed and cut into chunks
- 2 tablespoons olive oil
- 1 teaspoon dried thyme
- 1 teaspoon dried rosemary
- Salt and black pepper to taste

For the Baked Tofu Strips:

- 1 block (14 oz) extra-firm tofu, pressed and cut into strips
- 2 tablespoons soy sauce
- 1 tablespoon olive oil
- 1 teaspoon garlic powder
- 1 teaspoon smoked paprika
- Salt and black pepper to taste

Instructions:

1. Preheat your oven to 425°F (220°C). Grease a baking tray with cooking spray or olive oil.
2. In a bowl, toss the potato chunks with olive oil, dried thyme, dried rosemary, salt, and black pepper until well coated. Spread them out in a single layer on one side of the prepared baking tray.
3. In another bowl, marinate the tofu strips in soy sauce, olive oil, garlic powder, smoked paprika, salt, and black pepper for about 15 minutes.
4. Arrange the marinated tofu strips on the other side of the

baking tray, ensuring they are in a single layer.

5. Roast in the preheated oven for 25-30 minutes, or until the potatoes are tender and golden brown, and the tofu strips are crispy on the outside.
6. Once cooked, remove from the oven and let the potatoes and tofu strips cool for a few minutes before serving.
7. Serve the herb-roasted potatoes with baked tofu strips hot, accompanied by a side salad or steamed vegetables.
8. Enjoy your delicious and nutritious herb-roasted potatoes with baked tofu strips!

B. Vegan Chickpea and Potato Tray with Mediterranean Flavors
Ingredients:
For the Chickpeas and Potatoes:

- 1 can (15 oz) chickpeas, drained and rinsed
- 4 medium potatoes, washed and cut into chunks
- 2 tablespoons olive oil
- 1 teaspoon dried oregano
- 1 teaspoon dried thyme
- 1 teaspoon smoked paprika
- Salt and black pepper to taste

For the Mediterranean Flavors:

- 1/2 cup sun-dried tomatoes, chopped
- 1/4 cup Kalamata olives, pitted and sliced
- 2 tablespoons capers
- 2 tablespoons fresh parsley, chopped
- Lemon wedges, for serving

Instructions:

1. Preheat your oven to 425°F (220°C). Grease a baking tray with

cooking spray or olive oil.

2. In a large bowl, toss the chickpeas and potato chunks with olive oil, dried oregano, dried thyme, smoked paprika, salt, and black pepper until well coated.

3. Spread the seasoned chickpeas and potatoes out in a single layer on the prepared baking tray.

4. Roast in the preheated oven for 25-30 minutes, or until the potatoes are tender and golden brown, stirring halfway through cooking.

5. Once cooked, remove from the oven and sprinkle sun-dried tomatoes, Kalamata olives, capers, and fresh parsley over the roasted chickpeas and potatoes.

6. Serve the vegan chickpea and potato tray hot, accompanied by lemon wedges for squeezing over the dish.

7. Enjoy the Mediterranean flavors of this vegan chickpea and potato tray as a satisfying and nutritious meal!

C. Stuffed Portobello Mushrooms with Roasted Potato Slices
Ingredients:
For the Stuffed Portobello Mushrooms:

- 4 large portobello mushrooms, stems removed
- 1 tablespoon olive oil
- 2 cloves garlic, minced
- 1 small onion, finely chopped
- 1 cup spinach, chopped
- 1/2 cup sun-dried tomatoes, chopped
- 1/4 cup bread crumbs
- 1/4 cup vegan parmesan cheese (optional)
- Salt and black pepper to taste
- Fresh parsley, chopped (for garnish)

For the Roasted Potato Slices:

- 4 medium potatoes, washed and thinly sliced
- 2 tablespoons olive oil
- 1 teaspoon dried thyme
- 1 teaspoon dried rosemary
- Salt and black pepper to taste

Instructions:

1. Preheat your oven to 400°F (200°C). Grease a baking tray with cooking spray or olive oil.
2. Place the portobello mushrooms on the prepared baking tray, gill side up.
3. In a skillet, heat olive oil over medium heat. Add minced garlic and chopped onion, and sauté until softened, about 3-4 minutes.
4. Add chopped spinach and sun-dried tomatoes to the skillet, and cook until the spinach is wilted. Season with salt and black pepper to taste.
5. Remove the skillet from heat and stir in bread crumbs and vegan parmesan cheese (if using).
6. Spoon the spinach mixture into the hollowed-out portobello mushrooms, dividing it evenly among them.
7. In a separate bowl, toss the potato slices with olive oil, dried thyme, dried rosemary, salt, and black pepper until well coated.
8. Arrange the seasoned potato slices around the stuffed portobello mushrooms on the baking tray.
9. Roast in the preheated oven for 20-25 minutes, or until the potatoes are tender and golden brown, and the mushrooms are cooked through.
10. Once cooked, remove from the oven and let the stuffed portobello mushrooms and roasted potato slices cool for a few minutes before serving.
11. Garnish the stuffed portobello mushrooms with chopped fresh

parsley before serving.

12. Serve the stuffed portobello mushrooms with roasted potato slices hot, accompanied by a side salad or your favorite dipping sauce.

13. Enjoy your delightful stuffed portobello mushrooms with roasted potato slices for a satisfying and flavorful vegan meal!

Chapter (5) Side Dishes to Complement Potato Tray with Chicken

A. Fresh Garden Salad with Lemon Vinaigrette

Ingredients:

For the Salad:

- Mixed greens (such as lettuce, spinach, arugula)
- Cherry tomatoes, halved
- Cucumber, sliced
- Red onion, thinly sliced
- Carrots, shredded
- Any other desired vegetables

For the Lemon Vinaigrette:

- 1/4 cup extra virgin olive oil
- 2 tablespoons fresh lemon juice
- 1 teaspoon Dijon mustard
- 1 teaspoon honey or maple syrup (optional)
- Salt and black pepper to taste

Instructions:

1. In a large bowl, combine the mixed greens, cherry tomatoes, cucumber, red onion, carrots, and any other desired vegetables.
2. In a small bowl, whisk together the extra virgin olive oil, fresh lemon juice, Dijon mustard, honey or maple syrup (if using), salt, and black pepper until well combined.
3. Pour the lemon vinaigrette over the salad and toss gently to coat.
4. Serve the fresh garden salad alongside the potato tray with chicken.

5. Enjoy the refreshing and tangy flavors of the fresh garden salad with lemon vinaigrette!

B. Garlic Butter Green Beans
Ingredients:

- 1 pound green beans, trimmed
- 2 tablespoons butter (or vegan butter)
- 2 cloves garlic, minced
- Salt and black pepper to taste
- Lemon wedges (optional, for serving)

Instructions:

1. Bring a pot of salted water to a boil. Add the green beans and cook for 3-4 minutes, or until tender-crisp. Drain and set aside.
2. In a large skillet, melt the butter over medium heat. Add the minced garlic and sauté for 1-2 minutes, or until fragrant.
3. Add the cooked green beans to the skillet and toss to coat in the garlic butter. Season with salt and black pepper to taste.
4. Cook for an additional 2-3 minutes, stirring occasionally, until the green beans are heated through and coated in the garlic butter.
5. Transfer the garlic butter green beans to a serving dish.
6. Serve the garlic butter green beans with lemon wedges on the side, if desired.
7. Enjoy the crisp and flavorful garlic butter green beans as a perfect complement to the potato tray with chicken!

C. Grilled Vegetables with Balsamic Glaze
Ingredients:
For the Grilled Vegetables:

- Assorted vegetables (such as bell peppers, zucchini, eggplant, mushrooms, cherry tomatoes, red onion), sliced or halved
- 2 tablespoons olive oil
- Salt and black pepper to taste
- Fresh herbs (such as thyme, rosemary, or basil), chopped for garnish

For the Balsamic Glaze:

- 1/2 cup balsamic vinegar
- 2 tablespoons honey or maple syrup (optional)
- Salt and black pepper to taste

Instructions:

1. Preheat your grill to medium-high heat.
2. In a large bowl, toss the assorted vegetables with olive oil, salt, and black pepper until well coated.
3. Grill the vegetables on the preheated grill until they are tender and have grill marks, about 3-5 minutes per side depending on the thickness of the vegetables.
4. While the vegetables are grilling, prepare the balsamic glaze. In a small saucepan, combine the balsamic vinegar and honey or maple syrup (if using). Bring to a simmer over medium heat.
5. Cook, stirring occasionally, until the mixture has thickened and reduced by half, about 8-10 minutes. Season with salt and black pepper to taste.
6. Once the vegetables are grilled to your liking, transfer them to a serving platter.
7. Drizzle the balsamic glaze over the grilled vegetables.
8. Garnish with chopped fresh herbs, if desired.
9. Serve the grilled vegetables with balsamic glaze alongside the potato tray with chicken.

10. Enjoy the smoky flavors of the grilled vegetables complemented by the sweet and tangy balsamic glaze!

D. Creamy Coleslaw
Ingredients:

- 1/2 small green cabbage, thinly sliced
- 1/2 small red cabbage, thinly sliced
- 2 carrots, grated
- 1/2 cup vegan mayonnaise
- 2 tablespoons apple cider vinegar
- 1 tablespoon Dijon mustard
- 1 tablespoon maple syrup or honey
- Salt and black pepper to taste
- Fresh parsley or cilantro, chopped for garnish (optional)

Instructions:

1. In a large bowl, combine the thinly sliced green cabbage, red cabbage, and grated carrots.
2. In a small bowl, whisk together the vegan mayonnaise, apple cider vinegar, Dijon mustard, maple syrup or honey, salt, and black pepper until smooth.
3. Pour the dressing over the cabbage and carrots, and toss until evenly coated.
4. Cover the bowl and refrigerate the coleslaw for at least 30 minutes to allow the flavors to meld.
5. Before serving, give the coleslaw a final toss and adjust the seasoning if needed.
6. Transfer the creamy coleslaw to a serving bowl and garnish with chopped fresh parsley or cilantro, if desired.
7. Serve the creamy coleslaw as a refreshing side dish alongside the potato tray with chicken.

8. Enjoy the crisp and creamy texture of this classic coleslaw!

E. Homemade Bread or Rolls
Ingredients:

- 4 cups all-purpose flour, plus extra for dusting
- 2 1/4 teaspoons active dry yeast (1 packet)
- 1 1/2 cups warm water (110°F/45°C)
- 2 tablespoons granulated sugar
- 2 tablespoons olive oil
- 1 teaspoon salt
- 1 tablespoon melted vegan butter (optional, for brushing)

Instructions:

1. In a large mixing bowl, combine the warm water and sugar. Stir until the sugar dissolves. Sprinkle the active dry yeast over the water and let it sit for about 5-10 minutes, or until foamy.
2. Add the olive oil and salt to the yeast mixture and stir to combine.
3. Gradually add the flour, 1 cup at a time, stirring until a dough forms.
4. Turn the dough out onto a lightly floured surface and knead for about 8-10 minutes, or until the dough is smooth and elastic. You can also use a stand mixer fitted with a dough hook for kneading.
5. Shape the dough into a ball and place it in a lightly greased bowl. Cover the bowl with a clean kitchen towel or plastic wrap and let the dough rise in a warm, draft-free place for about 1 hour, or until doubled in size.
6. Punch down the risen dough to release the air bubbles. Turn the dough out onto a lightly floured surface and divide it into 12 equal portions.

7. Shape each portion of dough into a ball and place them on a baking sheet lined with parchment paper, spacing them a few inches apart.

8. Cover the dough balls with a clean kitchen towel and let them rise for another 30-45 minutes, or until doubled in size.

9. Preheat your oven to 375°F (190°C).

10. Once the dough balls have risen, brush the tops with melted vegan butter, if desired.

11. Bake in the preheated oven for 15-20 minutes, or until the rolls are golden brown and sound hollow when tapped on the bottom.

12. Remove the rolls from the oven and let them cool on a wire rack for a few minutes before serving.

13. Serve the homemade bread rolls warm with butter or alongside the potato tray with chicken.

14. Enjoy the soft and fluffy texture of these delicious homemade bread rolls!

Chapter (6) Desserts for a Complete Meal

A. Classic Apple Crisp
Ingredients:
For the Apple Filling:

- 6 cups apples, peeled, cored, and sliced (such as Granny Smith or Honeycrisp)
- 1/4 cup granulated sugar
- 1 tablespoon lemon juice
- 1 teaspoon ground cinnamon
- 1/4 teaspoon ground nutmeg
- 1/4 teaspoon salt

For the Crumble Topping:

- 1 cup old-fashioned rolled oats
- 1/2 cup all-purpose flour
- 1/2 cup brown sugar
- 1/2 teaspoon ground cinnamon
- 1/4 teaspoon salt
- 1/2 cup unsalted butter, cold and cubed

Instructions:

1. Preheat your oven to 350°F (175°C). Grease a 9x13-inch baking dish with butter or cooking spray.
2. In a large bowl, toss the sliced apples with granulated sugar, lemon juice, ground cinnamon, ground nutmeg, and salt until evenly coated. Transfer the apple mixture to the prepared baking dish, spreading it out in an even layer.
3. In another bowl, combine rolled oats, all-purpose flour, brown sugar, ground cinnamon, and salt. Add the cold cubed butter

and use your fingers or a pastry cutter to cut the butter into the dry ingredients until the mixture resembles coarse crumbs.

4. Sprinkle the crumble topping evenly over the apple mixture in the baking dish.
5. Bake in the preheated oven for 40-45 minutes, or until the topping is golden brown and the apples are tender and bubbling.
6. Remove from the oven and let the apple crisp cool for a few minutes before serving.
7. Serve the classic apple crisp warm, optionally topped with vanilla ice cream or whipped cream.
8. Enjoy the comforting flavors of this delicious classic apple crisp!

B. Chocolate Lava Cake

Ingredients:

- 4 ounces (120g) dark chocolate, chopped
- 1/2 cup (115g) unsalted butter
- 1/4 cup (50g) granulated sugar
- 2 large eggs
- 2 large egg yolks
- 1 teaspoon vanilla extract
- 1/4 cup (30g) all-purpose flour
- Pinch of salt
- Powdered sugar, for dusting (optional)
- Vanilla ice cream or whipped cream, for serving (optional)

Instructions:

1. Preheat your oven to 425°F (220°C). Grease four ramekins with butter and dust with cocoa powder or flour.
2. In a microwave-safe bowl, melt the chopped dark chocolate and unsalted butter together in the microwave in 30-second

intervals, stirring until smooth.

3. In a separate bowl, whisk together granulated sugar, eggs, egg yolks, and vanilla extract until well combined.
4. Gradually pour the melted chocolate mixture into the egg mixture, whisking constantly until smooth.
5. Sift in all-purpose flour and a pinch of salt, and gently fold until just combined.
6. Divide the batter evenly among the prepared ramekins.
7. Place the ramekins on a baking sheet and bake in the preheated oven for 12-14 minutes, or until the edges are set but the center is still soft.
8. Remove from the oven and let the chocolate lava cakes cool for 1-2 minutes.
9. Carefully run a knife around the edge of each ramekin to loosen the cakes, then invert them onto serving plates.
10. Dust with powdered sugar, if desired, and serve immediately with vanilla ice cream or whipped cream.
11. Enjoy the irresistible molten chocolate center of these decadent chocolate lava cakes!

C. Fresh Fruit Salad with Honey Yogurt Dressing
Ingredients:
For the Fruit Salad:

- Assorted fresh fruits (such as strawberries, blueberries, raspberries, blackberries, grapes, pineapple, mango, kiwi, oranges), washed, peeled, and chopped as needed

For the Honey Yogurt Dressing:

- 1/2 cup plain Greek yogurt
- 2 tablespoons honey
- 1 tablespoon lemon juice

- 1 teaspoon vanilla extract

Instructions:

1. In a large bowl, combine the assorted fresh fruits.
2. In a small bowl, whisk together plain Greek yogurt, honey, lemon juice, and vanilla extract until smooth.
3. Pour the honey yogurt dressing over the fresh fruits and gently toss until evenly coated.
4. Serve the fresh fruit salad immediately or refrigerate until ready to serve.
5. Enjoy the vibrant flavors and refreshing taste of this fresh fruit salad with honey yogurt dressing!
6. These desserts are sure to satisfy your sweet tooth and provide a delightful ending to your meal. Let me know if you need further assistance or have any questions!

Chapter (7) One-Pan Wonders: Chicken and Potato Tray with Additional Ingredients

A. Sheet Pan Chicken and Potato with Roasted Vegetables

Ingredients:

For the Chicken and Potatoes:

- 4 bone-in, skin-on chicken thighs
- 4 medium potatoes, washed and cut into chunks
- 2 tablespoons olive oil
- 1 teaspoon garlic powder
- 1 teaspoon paprika
- Salt and black pepper to taste

For the Roasted Vegetables:

- Assorted vegetables (such as bell peppers, broccoli, cauliflower, carrots, Brussels sprouts), washed and chopped
- 2 tablespoons olive oil
- Salt and black pepper to taste
- Optional seasonings: garlic powder, dried herbs (such as thyme, rosemary, or oregano)

Instructions:

1. Preheat your oven to 425°F (220°C). Grease a large baking sheet with cooking spray or olive oil.
2. In a bowl, toss the chicken thighs and potato chunks with olive oil, garlic powder, paprika, salt, and black pepper until evenly coated.
3. Arrange the chicken thighs and potatoes on one side of the prepared baking sheet.

4. In another bowl, toss the assorted vegetables with olive oil, salt, black pepper, and any desired seasonings until well coated.

5. Spread the seasoned vegetables out on the other side of the baking sheet, ensuring they are in a single layer.

6. Roast in the preheated oven for 30-35 minutes, or until the chicken is cooked through (internal temperature of 165°F/ 74°C) and the potatoes are tender and golden brown, and the vegetables are roasted and caramelized, stirring the vegetables halfway through cooking.

7. Once cooked, remove from the oven and let the chicken, potatoes, and roasted vegetables rest for a few minutes before serving.

8. Serve the sheet pan chicken and potato with roasted vegetables hot, garnished with fresh herbs if desired.

9. Enjoy the flavorful and convenient one-pan meal of sheet pan chicken and potato with roasted vegetables!

B. Chicken and Potato Tray with Bacon and Cheddar
Ingredients:
For the Chicken and Potatoes:

- 4 boneless, skinless chicken breasts
- 4 medium potatoes, washed and cut into chunks
- 4 slices bacon, cooked and crumbled
- 1 cup shredded cheddar cheese
- 2 tablespoons olive oil
- 1 teaspoon garlic powder
- 1 teaspoon onion powder
- Salt and black pepper to taste

Instructions:

1. Preheat your oven to 400°F (200°C). Grease a large baking dish with cooking spray or olive oil.
2. In a bowl, toss the chicken breasts and potato chunks with olive oil, garlic powder, onion powder, salt, and black pepper until evenly coated.
3. Arrange the seasoned chicken breasts and potatoes in a single layer in the prepared baking dish.
4. Sprinkle the cooked and crumbled bacon evenly over the chicken and potatoes.
5. Top each chicken breast with shredded cheddar cheese.
6. Bake in the preheated oven for 25-30 minutes, or until the chicken is cooked through (internal temperature of 165°F/74°C) and the potatoes are tender and golden brown.
7. Once cooked, remove from the oven and let the chicken and potatoes rest for a few minutes before serving.
8. Serve the chicken and potato tray with bacon and cheddar hot, accompanied by a side salad or your favorite vegetables.
9. Enjoy the indulgent flavors of this chicken and potato tray with bacon and cheddar!

C. Mediterranean-inspired Chicken, Potato, and Artichoke Heart Tray
Ingredients:
For the Chicken, Potatoes, and Artichoke Hearts:

- 4 bone-in, skin-on chicken thighs
- 4 medium potatoes, washed and cut into chunks
- 1 can (14 oz) artichoke hearts, drained and halved
- 2 tablespoons olive oil
- 2 cloves garlic, minced
- 1 teaspoon dried oregano
- 1 teaspoon dried basil
- 1/2 teaspoon dried thyme

- Salt and black pepper to taste

For the Mediterranean Flavors:

- 1/4 cup Kalamata olives, pitted
- 2 tablespoons capers
- 1 lemon, sliced
- Fresh parsley, chopped for garnish

Instructions:

1. Preheat your oven to 425°F (220°C). Grease a large baking dish with cooking spray or olive oil.
2. In a small bowl, mix together olive oil, minced garlic, dried oregano, dried basil, dried thyme, salt, and black pepper.
3. Place the chicken thighs, potato chunks, and halved artichoke hearts in the prepared baking dish. Drizzle the olive oil mixture over them and toss to coat evenly.
4. Arrange the lemon slices, Kalamata olives, and capers around the chicken, potatoes, and artichoke hearts.
5. Bake in the preheated oven for 35-40 minutes, or until the chicken is cooked through (internal temperature of 165°F/ 74°C) and the potatoes are tender, flipping the chicken and stirring the potatoes halfway through cooking.
6. Once cooked, remove from the oven and let the chicken, potatoes, and artichoke hearts rest for a few minutes before serving.
7. Garnish with fresh chopped parsley before serving.
8. Serve the Mediterranean-inspired chicken, potato, and artichoke heart tray hot, accompanied by a side salad or steamed vegetables.
9. Enjoy the aromatic flavors of this Mediterranean-inspired one-pan meal!

D. Tex-Mex Chicken and Potato Tray with Corn and Black Beans
Ingredients:
For the Chicken and Potatoes:

- 4 boneless, skinless chicken breasts
- 4 medium potatoes, washed and cut into chunks
- 2 tablespoons olive oil
- 1 teaspoon chili powder
- 1 teaspoon ground cumin
- 1/2 teaspoon smoked paprika
- Salt and black pepper to taste

Additional Ingredients:

- 1 cup corn kernels (fresh, canned, or frozen)
- 1 cup canned black beans, drained and rinsed
- 1/2 cup shredded Mexican cheese blend
- Fresh cilantro, chopped for garnish

Instructions:

1. Preheat your oven to 400°F (200°C). Grease a large baking dish with cooking spray or olive oil.
2. In a small bowl, mix together olive oil, chili powder, ground cumin, smoked paprika, salt, and black pepper.
3. Place the chicken breasts and potato chunks in the prepared baking dish. Drizzle the olive oil mixture over them and toss to coat evenly.
4. Spread the corn kernels and black beans evenly over the chicken and potatoes.
5. Bake in the preheated oven for 25-30 minutes, or until the chicken is cooked through (internal temperature of 165°F/ 74°C) and the potatoes are tender, stirring the potatoes halfway through cooking.

6. Once cooked, remove from the oven and sprinkle shredded Mexican cheese blend over the chicken, potatoes, corn, and black beans.
7. Return to the oven and bake for an additional 3-5 minutes, or until the cheese is melted and bubbly.
8. Once melted, remove from the oven and let the Tex-Mex chicken and potato tray rest for a few minutes before serving.
9. Garnish with fresh chopped cilantro before serving.
10. Serve the Tex-Mex chicken and potato tray hot, accompanied by tortilla chips, salsa, guacamole, or your favorite Tex-Mex condiments.
11. Enjoy the bold flavors of this Tex-Mex-inspired one-pan meal!

Chapter (8) Global Flavors: Chicken and Potato Tray with International Influences

A. Spanish-Inspired Chicken and Potato Tray with Chorizo and Paprika

Ingredients:

For the Chicken and Potatoes:

- 4 bone-in, skin-on chicken thighs
- 4 medium potatoes, washed and cut into chunks
- 4 oz Spanish chorizo, sliced
- 2 tablespoons olive oil
- 2 cloves garlic, minced
- 1 teaspoon smoked paprika
- 1/2 teaspoon Spanish paprika (optional)
- Salt and black pepper to taste

For the Spanish Flavors:

- 1 onion, sliced
- 1 red bell pepper, sliced
- 1 yellow bell pepper, sliced
- Fresh parsley, chopped for garnish

Instructions:

1. Preheat your oven to 425°F (220°C). Grease a large baking dish with cooking spray or olive oil.
2. In a small bowl, mix together olive oil, minced garlic, smoked paprika, Spanish paprika (if using), salt, and black pepper.
3. Place the chicken thighs and potato chunks in the prepared baking dish. Drizzle the olive oil mixture over them and toss to coat evenly.

4. Scatter the sliced Spanish chorizo, onion, red bell pepper, and yellow bell pepper around the chicken and potatoes.
5. Bake in the preheated oven for 35-40 minutes, or until the chicken is cooked through (internal temperature of 165°F/74°C) and the potatoes are tender, stirring halfway through cooking.
6. Once cooked, remove from the oven and let the chicken, potatoes, chorizo, and vegetables rest for a few minutes before serving.
7. Garnish with fresh chopped parsley before serving.
8. Serve the Spanish-inspired chicken and potato tray hot, accompanied by crusty bread or a side salad.
9. Enjoy the rich and smoky flavors of this Spanish-inspired one-pan meal!

B. French-style Coq au Vin with Potato Medley
Ingredients:
For the Chicken and Potatoes:

- 4 bone-in, skin-on chicken thighs
- 4 medium potatoes, washed and cut into chunks
- 2 tablespoons olive oil
- Salt and black pepper to taste

For the Coq au Vin Sauce:

- 4 slices bacon, chopped
- 1 onion, chopped
- 2 cloves garlic, minced
- 1 carrot, chopped
- 1 celery stalk, chopped
- 8 oz mushrooms, sliced
- 1 cup red wine (such as Pinot Noir or Burgundy)

- 1 cup chicken broth
- 2 tablespoons tomato paste
- 2 teaspoons fresh thyme leaves
- Salt and black pepper to taste
- Fresh parsley, chopped for garnish

Instructions:

1. Preheat your oven to 375°F (190°C). Grease a large baking dish with cooking spray or olive oil.
2. Season the chicken thighs and potato chunks with salt and black pepper. Place them in the prepared baking dish.
3. In a skillet, cook the chopped bacon over medium heat until crisp. Remove the bacon from the skillet and set aside, leaving the rendered fat in the skillet.
4. In the same skillet, add the chopped onion, garlic, carrot, celery, and mushrooms. Sauté until the vegetables are softened, about 5-7 minutes.
5. Pour in the red wine and chicken broth, and stir in the tomato paste and fresh thyme leaves. Bring the mixture to a simmer and cook for another 5 minutes.
6. Pour the Coq au Vin sauce over the chicken and potatoes in the baking dish.
7. Cover the baking dish with foil and bake in the preheated oven for 40-45 minutes, or until the chicken is cooked through (internal temperature of 165°F/74°C) and the potatoes are tender.
8. Once cooked, remove from the oven and let the Coq au Vin with potato medley rest for a few minutes before serving.
9. Garnish with chopped fresh parsley and the cooked bacon pieces before serving.
10. Serve the French-style Coq au Vin hot, accompanied by crusty French bread or rice.

11. Enjoy the comforting and aromatic flavors of this French-inspired one-pan meal!

C. Greek Lemon Chicken and Potato Tray with Tzatziki Sauce
Ingredients:
For the Greek Lemon Chicken and Potatoes:

- 4 bone-in, skin-on chicken thighs
- 4 medium potatoes, washed and cut into chunks
- 2 tablespoons olive oil
- 2 cloves garlic, minced
- Zest and juice of 1 lemon
- 1 teaspoon dried oregano
- 1/2 teaspoon dried thyme
- Salt and black pepper to taste

For the Tzatziki Sauce:

- 1 cup Greek yogurt
- 1 cucumber, grated and squeezed to remove excess moisture
- 1 clove garlic, minced
- 1 tablespoon fresh lemon juice
- 1 tablespoon chopped fresh dill (or 1 teaspoon dried dill)
- Salt and black pepper to taste

Instructions:

1. Preheat your oven to 425°F (220°C). Grease a large baking dish with cooking spray or olive oil.
2. In a small bowl, mix together olive oil, minced garlic, lemon zest, lemon juice, dried oregano, dried thyme, salt, and black pepper.
3. Place the chicken thighs and potato chunks in the prepared baking dish. Drizzle the olive oil mixture over them and toss to

coat evenly.

4. Bake in the preheated oven for 35-40 minutes, or until the chicken is cooked through (internal temperature of 165°F/ 74°C) and the potatoes are tender, flipping the chicken and stirring the potatoes halfway through cooking.

5. While the chicken and potatoes are baking, prepare the tzatziki sauce. In a bowl, combine Greek yogurt, grated cucumber, minced garlic, fresh lemon juice, chopped fresh dill, salt, and black pepper. Mix well and refrigerate until ready to serve.

6. Once cooked, remove from the oven and let the chicken and potatoes rest for a few minutes before serving.

7. Serve the Greek lemon chicken and potato tray hot, accompanied by the tzatziki sauce on the side.

8. Enjoy the vibrant flavors of this Greek-inspired one-pan meal!

D. Korean BBQ Chicken with Soy-Glazed Potatoes
Ingredients:
For the Korean BBQ Chicken:

- 4 boneless, skinless chicken breasts
- 2 tablespoons soy sauce
- 2 tablespoons honey
- 1 tablespoon sesame oil
- 2 cloves garlic, minced
- 1 teaspoon grated fresh ginger
- 1 teaspoon gochujang (Korean chili paste) or sriracha (optional for spice)
- Sesame seeds and chopped green onions for garnish

For the Soy-Glazed Potatoes:

- 4 medium potatoes, washed and cut into chunks
- 2 tablespoons soy sauce

- 1 tablespoon honey
- 1 tablespoon olive oil
- 1 teaspoon sesame seeds

Instructions:

1. Preheat your oven to 425°F (220°C). Grease a large baking dish with cooking spray or olive oil.
2. In a bowl, whisk together soy sauce, honey, sesame oil, minced garlic, grated fresh ginger, and gochujang (if using) to make the Korean BBQ marinade.
3. Place the chicken breasts in the marinade, ensuring they are coated evenly. Let them marinate for at least 30 minutes in the refrigerator.
4. In another bowl, toss the potato chunks with soy sauce, honey, olive oil, and sesame seeds to make the soy-glazed potatoes.
5. Place the marinated chicken breasts and potato chunks in the prepared baking dish.
6. Bake in the preheated oven for 25-30 minutes, or until the chicken is cooked through (internal temperature of 165°F/ 74°C) and the potatoes are tender and caramelized, flipping the chicken and stirring the potatoes halfway through cooking.
7. Once cooked, remove from the oven and let the Korean BBQ chicken and soy-glazed potatoes rest for a few minutes before serving.
8. Garnish the chicken with sesame seeds and chopped green onions before serving.
9. Serve the Korean BBQ chicken with soy-glazed potatoes hot, accompanied by steamed rice and your favorite vegetables.
10. Enjoy the bold and savory flavors of this Korean-inspired one-pan meal!

Chapter (9) Brunch Delights: Chicken and Potato Tray for Morning Feasts

A. Chicken and Potato Breakfast Hash with Sunny-Side-Up Eggs
Ingredients:
For the Chicken and Potato Hash:

- 4 boneless, skinless chicken breasts, diced
- 4 medium potatoes, peeled and diced
- 1 onion, diced
- 1 bell pepper, diced
- 2 cloves garlic, minced
- 2 tablespoons olive oil
- Salt and black pepper to taste
- 1 teaspoon paprika
- 1 teaspoon dried thyme
- 1/2 teaspoon garlic powder
- 1/2 teaspoon onion powder
- Fresh parsley, chopped for garnish

For Serving:

- Eggs (1-2 per person)
- Cooking spray or butter for frying eggs

Instructions:

1. Preheat your oven to 400°F (200°C). Grease a large baking dish with cooking spray or olive oil.
2. In a large bowl, combine diced chicken breasts, diced potatoes, diced onion, diced bell pepper, minced garlic, olive oil, salt, black pepper, paprika, dried thyme, garlic powder, and onion powder. Toss until everything is evenly coated.

3. Spread the chicken and potato mixture onto the prepared baking dish in an even layer.
4. Bake in the preheated oven for 25-30 minutes, or until the chicken is cooked through and the potatoes are tender and golden brown, stirring halfway through cooking.
5. While the hash is baking, cook the sunny-side-up eggs in a skillet over medium heat until the whites are set but the yolks are still runny.
6. Once the chicken and potato hash is cooked, remove from the oven and divide onto plates.
7. Top each portion with a sunny-side-up egg and garnish with chopped fresh parsley.
8. Serve the chicken and potato breakfast hash hot, with toast or crusty bread on the side if desired.
9. Enjoy this hearty and flavorful brunch delight!

B. Chicken and Potato Breakfast Burrito Bake
Ingredients:

- 4 boneless, skinless chicken breasts, cooked and shredded
- 4 medium potatoes, peeled and diced
- 1 onion, diced
- 1 bell pepper, diced
- 8 large eggs
- 1 cup shredded cheddar cheese
- 1/4 cup milk
- Salt and black pepper to taste
- 1 teaspoon paprika
- 1 teaspoon dried thyme
- 1/2 teaspoon garlic powder
- 1/2 teaspoon onion powder
- Cooking spray or olive oil for greasing

Instructions:

1. Preheat your oven to 375°F (190°C). Grease a 9x13-inch baking dish with cooking spray or olive oil.
2. In a large skillet, cook the diced potatoes over medium heat until they are golden brown and cooked through. Add diced onion and bell pepper, and cook until softened.
3. In a large bowl, whisk together eggs, milk, shredded cheddar cheese, paprika, dried thyme, garlic powder, onion powder, salt, and black pepper.
4. Spread the cooked chicken, potato, onion, and bell pepper mixture evenly in the prepared baking dish.
5. Pour the egg mixture over the top, ensuring it covers the entire surface evenly.
6. Bake in the preheated oven for 25-30 minutes, or until the eggs are set and the top is golden brown.
7. Once cooked, remove from the oven and let it cool slightly before slicing into squares.
8. Serve the chicken and potato breakfast burrito bake hot, with salsa, sour cream, avocado slices, or your favorite toppings.
9. Enjoy this delicious and convenient brunch option!

C. Chicken and Potato Frittata with Spinach and Feta
Ingredients:

- 4 boneless, skinless chicken breasts, cooked and diced
- 4 medium potatoes, peeled and diced
- 1 onion, diced
- 2 cups fresh spinach leaves
- 6 large eggs
- 1/4 cup milk
- 1/2 cup crumbled feta cheese
- Salt and black pepper to taste

- 2 tablespoons olive oil
- Cooking spray for greasing

Instructions:

1. Preheat your oven to 375°F (190°C). Grease a 9-inch oven-safe skillet with cooking spray.
2. In a large skillet, heat olive oil over medium heat. Add diced potatoes and cook until they are golden brown and cooked through. Add diced onion and cook until softened.
3. Add diced cooked chicken and fresh spinach leaves to the skillet. Cook until the spinach wilts.
4. In a separate bowl, whisk together eggs, milk, crumbled feta cheese, salt, and black pepper.
5. Pour the egg mixture over the chicken, potato, onion, and spinach mixture in the skillet. Stir gently to combine.
6. Cook over medium heat for 2-3 minutes, allowing the edges to set.
7. Transfer the skillet to the preheated oven and bake for 20-25 minutes, or until the frittata is set in the center and golden brown on top.
8. Once cooked, remove from the oven and let it cool slightly before slicing into wedges.
9. Serve the chicken and potato frittata with spinach and feta hot, accompanied by a side salad or your favorite brunch sides.
10. Enjoy this flavorful and nutritious brunch option!

D. Chicken and Potato Breakfast Casserole with Cheese and Sausage
Ingredients:

- 4 boneless, skinless chicken breasts, cooked and shredded
- 4 medium potatoes, peeled and diced

- 1 onion, diced
- 1 bell pepper, diced
- 8 oz cooked breakfast sausage, crumbled
- 2 cups shredded cheddar cheese
- 8 large eggs
- 1 cup milk
- Salt and black pepper to taste
- Cooking spray for greasing

Instructions:

1. Preheat your oven to 375°F (190°C). Grease a 9x13-inch baking dish with cooking spray.
2. In a large skillet, cook diced potatoes over medium heat until they are golden brown and cooked through. Add diced onion and bell pepper, and cook until softened.
3. In a large bowl, whisk together eggs, milk, shredded cheddar cheese, salt, and black pepper.
4. Spread the cooked chicken, potato, onion, bell pepper, and crumbled breakfast sausage evenly in the prepared baking dish.
5. Pour the egg mixture over the top, ensuring it covers the entire surface evenly.
6. Bake in the preheated oven for 30-35 minutes, or until the eggs are set and the top is golden brown.
7. Once cooked, remove from the oven and let it cool slightly before slicing into squares.
8. Serve the chicken and potato breakfast casserole hot, with salsa, sour cream, avocado slices, or your favorite toppings.
9. Enjoy this comforting and satisfying brunch casserole!

Chapter (10) Kid-Friendly Creations: Chicken and Potato Tray for Picky Eaters

A. Crispy Chicken Tenders with Potato Wedges and Dipping Sauces
Ingredients:
For the Chicken Tenders:

- 1 lb chicken breast tenders
- 1 cup all-purpose flour
- 2 eggs, beaten
- 1 cup breadcrumbs
- 1 teaspoon paprika
- 1/2 teaspoon garlic powder
- Salt and pepper to taste
- Cooking spray

For the Potato Wedges:

- 4 medium potatoes, washed and cut into wedges
- 2 tablespoons olive oil
- 1 teaspoon garlic powder
- 1 teaspoon paprika
- Salt and pepper to taste

For Dipping Sauces (choose 2 or more):

- Ketchup
- Barbecue sauce
- Honey mustard
- Ranch dressing

Instructions:

1. Preheat your oven to 425°F (220°C). Line a baking sheet with parchment paper.
2. In three separate shallow dishes, place the flour in one, beaten eggs in another, and breadcrumbs mixed with paprika, garlic powder, salt, and pepper in the third.
3. Dredge each chicken tender in the flour, then dip into the beaten eggs, and finally coat with the breadcrumb mixture, pressing gently to adhere. Place the coated tenders on one side of the prepared baking sheet.
4. In a large bowl, toss the potato wedges with olive oil, garlic powder, paprika, salt, and pepper until evenly coated. Arrange the wedges on the other side of the baking sheet.
5. Bake in the preheated oven for 20-25 minutes, flipping the chicken tenders and stirring the potato wedges halfway through cooking, until the chicken is cooked through and the potatoes are golden and crispy.
6. While the chicken tenders and potato wedges are baking, prepare the dipping sauces by placing each sauce in separate small bowls.
7. Once cooked, remove from the oven and let cool slightly.
8. Serve the crispy chicken tenders with potato wedges hot, accompanied by the dipping sauces.
9. Enjoy this kid-friendly meal that's perfect for dipping and dunking!

B. Chicken and Potato Tray Pizza with Kid-Friendly Toppings
Ingredients:

- 1 lb pizza dough
- 1 cup marinara sauce
- 1 cup shredded mozzarella cheese
- 1 cup cooked, shredded chicken breast
- 1 cup diced cooked potatoes

- Kid-friendly toppings such as sliced olives, diced bell peppers, sliced mushrooms, and pepperoni (optional)

Instructions:

1. Preheat your oven to 425°F (220°C). Grease a baking sheet or pizza pan with cooking spray or olive oil.
2. Roll out the pizza dough on the prepared baking sheet to your desired thickness.
3. Spread marinara sauce evenly over the pizza dough, leaving a small border around the edges.
4. Sprinkle shredded mozzarella cheese over the sauce, then distribute the cooked chicken and diced potatoes evenly over the cheese.
5. Add any additional kid-friendly toppings of your choice, such as sliced olives, diced bell peppers, sliced mushrooms, or pepperoni.
6. Bake in the preheated oven for 15-20 minutes, or until the crust is golden brown and the cheese is melted and bubbly.
7. Once cooked, remove from the oven and let cool slightly before slicing into slices or squares.
8. Serve the chicken and potato tray pizza hot, accompanied by a side salad or fresh fruit.
9. Enjoy this customizable and fun meal that's sure to please even the pickiest eaters!

C. Chicken and Potato Tray Sliders with Mini Buns

Ingredients:

- 12 slider buns
- 12 cooked chicken breast slices (can use leftover rotisserie chicken)
- 12 cooked potato slices (can use leftover roasted potatoes)

- Condiments such as ketchup, mustard, and mayonnaise (optional)
- Lettuce leaves and tomato slices (optional)

Instructions:

1. Preheat your oven to 350°F (175°C).
2. Slice the slider buns in half horizontally and place the bottom halves on a baking sheet.
3. Layer each bottom half of the slider buns with a cooked chicken breast slice and a cooked potato slice.
4. Add condiments such as ketchup, mustard, and mayonnaise if desired.
5. Top each slider with lettuce leaves and tomato slices if desired.
6. Place the top halves of the slider buns on top of the fillings to complete the sliders.
7. Cover the baking sheet with aluminum foil and bake in the preheated oven for 10-15 minutes, or until the sliders are heated through and the buns are lightly toasted.
8. Once cooked, remove from the oven and let cool slightly before serving.
9. Serve the chicken and potato tray sliders hot, accompanied by potato chips or carrot sticks.
10. Enjoy these bite-sized sliders that are perfect for little hands!

D. Cheesy Chicken and Potato Quesadillas
Ingredients:

- 8 medium flour tortillas
- 2 cups cooked, shredded chicken breast
- 2 cups cooked diced potatoes
- 2 cups shredded cheddar cheese
- 1 cup salsa

- 1/4 cup chopped fresh cilantro (optional)
- Cooking spray

Instructions:

1. In a large bowl, mix together shredded chicken, diced potatoes, shredded cheddar cheese, salsa, and chopped fresh cilantro (if using).
2. Heat a large skillet over medium heat. Lightly coat one side of a flour tortilla with cooking spray and place it in the skillet, sprayed side down.
3. Spread a generous portion of the chicken and potato mixture over half of the tortilla.
4. Fold the other half of the tortilla over the filling to form a half-moon shape.
5. Cook the quesadilla for 2-3 minutes on each side, or until golden brown and crispy and the cheese is melted.
6. Repeat with the remaining tortillas and filling.
7. Once cooked, remove from the skillet and let cool slightly before slicing into wedges.
8. Serve the cheesy chicken and potato quesadillas hot, accompanied by sour cream, guacamole, or additional salsa for dipping.
9. Enjoy these cheesy and satisfying quesadillas that are sure to please even the pickiest eaters!

Chapter (11) Healthy Options: Lighter Chicken and Potato Tray Variations

A. Grilled Chicken and Sweet Potato Tray with Lemon-Herb Marinade

Ingredients:

For the Grilled Chicken and Sweet Potatoes:

- 4 boneless, skinless chicken breasts
- 2 large sweet potatoes, washed and sliced into rounds
- 2 tablespoons olive oil
- Salt and black pepper to taste

For the Lemon-Herb Marinade:

- 1/4 cup olive oil
- Juice and zest of 1 lemon
- 2 cloves garlic, minced
- 1 tablespoon fresh chopped herbs (such as rosemary, thyme, or parsley)
- Salt and black pepper to taste

Instructions:

1. In a small bowl, whisk together the ingredients for the lemon-herb marinade: olive oil, lemon juice, lemon zest, minced garlic, chopped herbs, salt, and black pepper.
2. Place the chicken breasts in a shallow dish or resealable plastic bag, and pour the marinade over them. Ensure the chicken is evenly coated. Marinate in the refrigerator for at least 30 minutes, or up to 4 hours.
3. Preheat your grill to medium-high heat. Brush the grill grates with oil to prevent sticking.

4. Remove the chicken breasts from the marinade and discard any excess marinade. Place the chicken breasts on one side of a large sheet pan.

5. Place the sliced sweet potatoes on the other side of the sheet pan. Drizzle them with olive oil and season with salt and black pepper.

6. Grill the chicken breasts and sweet potatoes for 6-8 minutes per side, or until the chicken is cooked through (internal temperature of 165°F/74°C) and the sweet potatoes are tender and lightly charred.

7. Once cooked, remove from the grill and let the chicken and sweet potatoes rest for a few minutes before serving.

8. Serve the grilled chicken and sweet potato tray hot, accompanied by a side salad or steamed vegetables.

9. Enjoy this light and flavorful meal that's perfect for a healthy dinner option!

B. Baked Chicken Breast with Quinoa-Stuffed Potatoes

Ingredients:

For the Baked Chicken Breast:

- 4 boneless, skinless chicken breasts
- 2 tablespoons olive oil
- 2 cloves garlic, minced
- 1 teaspoon dried herbs (such as oregano, thyme, or basil)
- Salt and black pepper to taste

For the Quinoa-Stuffed Potatoes:

- 4 medium potatoes, washed and scrubbed
- 1/2 cup cooked quinoa
- 1/4 cup diced bell pepper
- 1/4 cup diced cucumber

- 1/4 cup diced cherry tomatoes
- 2 tablespoons chopped fresh parsley
- 2 tablespoons lemon juice
- Salt and black pepper to taste

Instructions:

1. Preheat your oven to 400°F (200°C).
2. Pierce the potatoes with a fork several times. Place them directly on the oven rack and bake for 45-60 minutes, or until tender.
3. While the potatoes are baking, prepare the quinoa-stuffed filling. In a bowl, combine cooked quinoa, diced bell pepper, diced cucumber, diced cherry tomatoes, chopped fresh parsley, lemon juice, salt, and black pepper. Mix well and set aside.
4. In another bowl, whisk together olive oil, minced garlic, dried herbs, salt, and black pepper. Place the chicken breasts in a shallow dish or resealable plastic bag, and pour the marinade over them. Ensure the chicken is evenly coated. Marinate in the refrigerator for at least 30 minutes.
5. Once the potatoes are baked and tender, remove them from the oven and let them cool slightly. Cut a slit lengthwise in each potato, and fluff the insides with a fork.
6. Fill each potato with the quinoa-stuffed filling mixture.
7. Place the marinated chicken breasts on a baking sheet lined with parchment paper or aluminum foil.
8. Bake the chicken breasts in the preheated oven for 20-25 minutes, or until they are cooked through (internal temperature of 165°F/74°C) and golden brown.
9. Once cooked, remove the chicken breasts from the oven and let them rest for a few minutes before serving.
10. Serve the baked chicken breast with quinoa-stuffed potatoes hot, accompanied by a side salad or steamed vegetables.
11. Enjoy this nutritious and satisfying meal that's packed with

flavor!

C. Chicken and Potato Tray with Roasted Brussels Sprouts and Cauliflower

Ingredients:

- 4 boneless, skinless chicken breasts
- 4 medium potatoes, washed and cut into chunks
- 2 cups Brussels sprouts, trimmed and halved
- 2 cups cauliflower florets
- 2 tablespoons olive oil
- 2 cloves garlic, minced
- 1 teaspoon dried herbs (such as thyme or rosemary)
- Salt and black pepper to taste

Instructions:

1. Preheat your oven to 425°F (220°C). Grease a large baking sheet with cooking spray or olive oil.
2. In a small bowl, whisk together olive oil, minced garlic, dried herbs, salt, and black pepper.
3. Place the chicken breasts and potato chunks on one side of the prepared baking sheet.
4. Place the Brussels sprouts and cauliflower florets on the other side of the baking sheet.
5. Drizzle the olive oil mixture over the chicken, potatoes, Brussels sprouts, and cauliflower, and toss to coat evenly.
6. Bake in the preheated oven for 25-30 minutes, or until the chicken is cooked through (internal temperature of 165°F/ 74°C) and the potatoes are tender and golden brown, stirring the vegetables halfway through cooking.
7. Once cooked, remove from the oven and let the chicken and vegetables rest for a few minutes before serving.

8. Serve the chicken and potato tray with roasted Brussels sprouts and cauliflower hot, accompanied by a side of mixed greens or steamed quinoa.

9. Enjoy this wholesome and nutritious meal that's perfect for a light dinner option!

D. Herb-Crusted Chicken with Steamed Potato Slices and Asparagus Spears

Ingredients:

For the Herb-Crusted Chicken:

- 4 boneless, skinless chicken breasts
- 2 tablespoons Dijon mustard
- 1 tablespoon olive oil
- 1 cup breadcrumbs
- 1/4 cup grated Parmesan cheese
- 1 teaspoon dried herbs (such as basil, oregano, or thyme)
- Salt and black pepper to taste

For the Steamed Potato Slices and Asparagus Spears:

- 4 medium potatoes, washed and sliced into rounds
- 1 bunch asparagus spears, trimmed
- Salt and black pepper to taste

Instructions:

1. Preheat your oven to 400°F (200°C). Grease a large baking dish with cooking spray or olive oil.
2. In a small bowl, whisk together Dijon mustard and olive oil. Brush the mixture over both sides of each chicken breast.
3. In another bowl, combine breadcrumbs, grated Parmesan cheese, dried herbs, salt, and black pepper.
4. Dip each chicken breast into the breadcrumb mixture, pressing

gently to coat evenly. Place the coated chicken breasts in the prepared baking dish.

5. Arrange the sliced potato rounds and asparagus spears around the chicken breasts in the baking dish. Season the potatoes and asparagus with salt and black pepper to taste.

6. Cover the baking dish with aluminum foil and bake in the preheated oven for 25-30 minutes, or until the chicken is cooked through (internal temperature of 165°F/74°C) and the potatoes are tender, removing the foil during the last 10 minutes of baking to allow the breadcrumbs to crisp up.

7. Once cooked, remove from the oven and let the chicken and vegetables rest for a few minutes before serving.

8. Serve the herb-crusted chicken with steamed potato slices and asparagus spears hot, accompanied by a side of steamed green beans or a mixed salad.

9. Enjoy this light and flavorful meal that's perfect for a healthier dinner option!

Chapter (12) Special Occasion Splurges: Chicken and Potato Tray for Festive Gatherings

A. Holiday Roast Chicken with Garlic Mashed Potatoes

Roast Chicken Ingredients:

- 1 whole chicken (about 4-5 pounds), giblets removed
- 2 tablespoons olive oil
- 2 teaspoons salt
- 1 teaspoon black pepper
- 1 teaspoon dried thyme
- 1 teaspoon dried rosemary
- 1 teaspoon paprika
- 1 lemon, halved
- 4 cloves garlic, minced
- Fresh herbs (such as rosemary, thyme, and parsley) for garnish

Garlic Mashed Potatoes Ingredients:

- 4 large russet potatoes, peeled and quartered
- 4 cloves garlic, peeled
- 1/2 cup milk
- 4 tablespoons butter
- Salt and pepper to taste
- Chopped fresh parsley for garnish

Instructions:

1. Preheat your oven to 425°F (220°C). Place a roasting rack in a roasting pan.
2. Rinse the chicken under cold water and pat dry with paper towels. Place the chicken on the roasting rack.

3. In a small bowl, mix together olive oil, salt, black pepper, dried thyme, dried rosemary, and paprika. Rub the mixture all over the chicken, including under the skin.

4. Squeeze the lemon halves over the chicken, then place the lemon halves inside the cavity along with the minced garlic and a few sprigs of fresh herbs.

5. Roast the chicken in the preheated oven for about 1 hour and 15 minutes, or until the internal temperature reaches 165°F (74°C) when measured with a meat thermometer inserted into the thickest part of the thigh.

6. While the chicken is roasting, prepare the garlic mashed potatoes. Place the quartered potatoes and garlic cloves in a large pot and cover with cold water. Bring to a boil over high heat, then reduce the heat to medium and simmer for about 15-20 minutes, or until the potatoes are fork-tender.

7. Drain the potatoes and garlic, then return them to the pot. Add milk, butter, salt, and pepper to taste. Mash with a potato masher until smooth and creamy.

8. Once the chicken is done, remove it from the oven and let it rest for about 10-15 minutes before carving.

9. Serve the roast chicken with garlic mashed potatoes hot, garnished with chopped fresh parsley.

10. Enjoy this festive and comforting meal perfect for holiday gatherings!

B. Chicken and Potato Tray with Cranberry Glaze for Thanksgiving

Ingredients:

- 4 bone-in, skin-on chicken thighs
- 4 bone-in, skin-on chicken drumsticks
- 4 large potatoes, washed and cut into wedges
- 1 cup fresh or frozen cranberries

- 1/4 cup orange juice
- 1/4 cup honey
- 2 tablespoons balsamic vinegar
- 2 cloves garlic, minced
- 1 teaspoon dried thyme
- Salt and pepper to taste
- Chopped fresh parsley for garnish

Instructions:

1. Preheat your oven to 400°F (200°C). Grease a large baking dish with cooking spray or olive oil.
2. Season the chicken thighs and drumsticks with salt, pepper, and dried thyme. Place them in the prepared baking dish.
3. Arrange the potato wedges around the chicken pieces in the baking dish.
4. In a small saucepan, combine cranberries, orange juice, honey, balsamic vinegar, minced garlic, salt, and pepper. Bring to a simmer over medium heat and cook for about 5-7 minutes, or until the cranberries burst and the sauce thickens slightly.
5. Pour the cranberry glaze over the chicken and potatoes in the baking dish.
6. Bake in the preheated oven for about 45-50 minutes, or until the chicken is cooked through (internal temperature of 165°F/ 74°C) and the potatoes are tender, basting the chicken and potatoes with the glaze halfway through cooking.
7. Once cooked, remove from the oven and let it rest for a few minutes before serving.
8. Serve the chicken and potato tray with cranberry glaze hot, garnished with chopped fresh parsley.
9. Enjoy this festive twist on a classic chicken and potato tray, perfect for Thanksgiving celebrations!

C. Easter Herb-Roasted Chicken with Scalloped Potatoes
Ingredients:

- 1 whole chicken (about 4-5 pounds), giblets removed
- 2 tablespoons olive oil
- 2 teaspoons salt
- 1 teaspoon black pepper
- 1 teaspoon dried rosemary
- 1 teaspoon dried thyme
- 1 teaspoon dried oregano
- 4 large potatoes, peeled and thinly sliced
- 2 cups heavy cream
- 2 cloves garlic, minced
- Salt and pepper to taste
- Chopped fresh parsley for garnish

Instructions:

1. Preheat your oven to 425°F (220°C). Place a roasting rack in a roasting pan.
2. Rinse the chicken under cold water and pat dry with paper towels. Place the chicken on the roasting rack.
3. In a small bowl, mix together olive oil, salt, black pepper, dried rosemary, dried thyme, and dried oregano. Rub the mixture all over the chicken, including under the skin.
4. Roast the chicken in the preheated oven for about 1 hour and 15 minutes, or until the internal temperature reaches 165°F (74°C) when measured with a meat thermometer inserted into the thickest part of the thigh.
5. While the chicken is roasting, prepare the scalloped potatoes. In a saucepan, combine heavy cream, minced garlic, salt, and pepper. Bring to a simmer over medium heat, then remove from heat.

6. Grease a large baking dish with cooking spray or olive oil. Arrange the thinly sliced potatoes in layers in the baking dish, seasoning each layer with salt and pepper.
7. Pour the hot cream mixture over the potatoes in the baking dish.
8. Bake the scalloped potatoes in the preheated oven for about 45-50 minutes, or until the potatoes are tender and golden brown on top.
9. Once the chicken is done, remove it from the oven and let it rest for about 10-15 minutes before carving.
10. Serve the herb-roasted chicken with scalloped potatoes hot, garnished with chopped fresh parsley.
11. Enjoy this elegant and delicious meal perfect for Easter gatherings!

D. Wedding-worthy Chicken and Potato Tray with Champagne Cream Sauce

Ingredients:

- 4 boneless, skinless chicken breasts
- 4 large potatoes, washed and cut into chunks
- 2 cups Brussels sprouts, trimmed and halved
- 2 cups cauliflower florets
- 2 tablespoons olive oil
- 2 cloves garlic, minced
- 1 teaspoon dried herbs (such as thyme or rosemary)
- Salt and black pepper to taste

Champagne Cream Sauce Ingredients:

- 1 cup champagne or sparkling wine
- 1 cup heavy cream
- 2 tablespoons butter

- 2 cloves garlic, minced
- Salt and black pepper to taste
- Chopped fresh parsley for garnish

Instructions:

1. Preheat your oven to 425°F (220°C). Grease a large baking dish with cooking spray or olive oil.
2. Season the chicken breasts with salt, pepper, and dried herbs. Place them in the prepared baking dish.
3. Arrange the potato chunks, Brussels sprouts, and cauliflower florets around the chicken breasts in the baking dish.
4. Drizzle the olive oil over the chicken and vegetables, then sprinkle minced garlic, salt, and black pepper over them.
5. Bake in the preheated oven for about 25-30 minutes, or until the chicken is cooked through (internal temperature of 165°F/ 74°C) and the potatoes are tender, stirring the vegetables halfway through cooking.
6. While the chicken and potatoes are baking, prepare the champagne cream sauce. In a saucepan, combine champagne, heavy cream, minced garlic, salt, and black pepper. Bring to a simmer over medium heat and cook for about 10-15 minutes, or until the sauce thickens slightly.
7. Once the chicken and potatoes are done, remove them from the oven and let them rest for a few minutes before serving.
8. Serve the chicken and potato tray with champagne cream sauce hot, garnished with chopped fresh parsley.
9. Enjoy this decadent and luxurious meal perfect for special occasions like weddings or anniversaries!

Chapter (13) Leftover Transformations: Creative Uses for Chicken and Potato Tray Leftovers

A. Chicken and Potato Tray Stir-Fry with Mixed Vegetables
   Ingredients:

- Leftover cooked chicken and potatoes from the tray
- Assorted mixed vegetables (such as bell peppers, broccoli, carrots, snap peas)
- 2 tablespoons soy sauce
- 1 tablespoon oyster sauce
- 1 teaspoon sesame oil
- 1 teaspoon minced ginger
- 2 cloves garlic, minced
- Cooked rice or noodles for serving
- Green onions, sliced, for garnish

Instructions:

1. Heat a large skillet or wok over medium-high heat. Add a bit of oil.
2. Add minced ginger and garlic to the skillet, and sauté until fragrant, about 1 minute.
3. Add the mixed vegetables to the skillet and stir-fry until they are crisp-tender.
4. Add the leftover cooked chicken and potatoes to the skillet. Stir-fry until heated through.
5. In a small bowl, mix together soy sauce, oyster sauce, and sesame oil. Pour the sauce over the chicken, potatoes, and vegetables. Stir well to combine.
6. Continue to cook for another 2-3 minutes, until everything is

heated through and coated in the sauce.

7. Serve the stir-fry hot over cooked rice or noodles. Garnish with sliced green onions.

8. Enjoy this quick and flavorful transformation of your chicken and potato tray leftovers!

B. Chicken and Potato Tray Hash for Breakfast or Brunch

Ingredients:

- Leftover cooked chicken and potatoes from the tray
- 1 onion, diced
- 1 bell pepper, diced
- 2 cloves garlic, minced
- 2 tablespoons olive oil
- Salt and pepper to taste
- Eggs (optional)
- Chopped fresh parsley for garnish

Instructions:

1. Heat olive oil in a large skillet over medium heat. Add diced onion and bell pepper, and sauté until softened, about 5 minutes.

2. Add minced garlic to the skillet, and cook for another minute until fragrant.

3. Add the leftover cooked chicken and potatoes to the skillet. Season with salt and pepper to taste.

4. Cook, stirring occasionally, until everything is heated through and slightly crispy, about 10-12 minutes.

5. If desired, create wells in the hash mixture and crack eggs into the wells. Cover the skillet and cook until the eggs are set to your liking.

6. Sprinkle chopped fresh parsley over the hash before serving.

7. Serve the chicken and potato tray hash hot, optionally with toast or English muffins on the side.

8. Enjoy this hearty and satisfying breakfast or brunch option using your leftover chicken and potatoes!

C. Chicken and Potato Tray Soup with Broth and Fresh Herbs
Ingredients:

- Leftover cooked chicken and potatoes from the tray
- 4 cups chicken or vegetable broth
- 1 onion, diced
- 2 carrots, diced
- 2 celery stalks, diced
- 2 cloves garlic, minced
- 1 teaspoon dried thyme
- 1 teaspoon dried rosemary
- Salt and pepper to taste
- Chopped fresh parsley for garnish

Instructions:

1. In a large pot, heat a bit of oil over medium heat. Add diced onion, carrots, and celery, and sauté until softened, about 5 minutes.

2. Add minced garlic, dried thyme, and dried rosemary to the pot, and cook for another minute until fragrant.

3. Pour in the chicken or vegetable broth, and bring the mixture to a simmer.

4. Add the leftover cooked chicken and potatoes to the pot. Season with salt and pepper to taste.

5. Simmer the soup for about 15-20 minutes to allow the flavors to meld together.

6. Serve the chicken and potato tray soup hot, garnished with

chopped fresh parsley.

7. Enjoy this comforting and nourishing soup made from your leftover chicken and potatoes!

D. Chicken and Potato Tray Stuffed Peppers or Bellas
Ingredients:

- Leftover cooked chicken and potatoes from the tray
- Bell peppers or portobello mushrooms
- 1 onion, diced
- 2 cloves garlic, minced
- 1 cup cooked rice or quinoa
- 1/2 cup shredded cheese (such as cheddar or mozzarella)
- Salt and pepper to taste
- Chopped fresh herbs for garnish

Instructions:

1. Preheat your oven to 375°F (190°C).
2. Cut the tops off the bell peppers and remove the seeds and membranes. If using portobello mushrooms, remove the stems and scoop out the gills.
3. In a skillet, heat a bit of oil over medium heat. Add diced onion and minced garlic, and sauté until softened, about 5 minutes.
4. Add the leftover cooked chicken and potatoes to the skillet, and cook until heated through.
5. Stir in cooked rice or quinoa, and season with salt and pepper to taste.
6. Stuff the bell peppers or portobello mushrooms with the chicken and potato mixture. Place them in a baking dish.
7. Sprinkle shredded cheese over the stuffed peppers or mushrooms.
8. Bake in the preheated oven for about 20-25 minutes, or until

the peppers or mushrooms are tender and the cheese is melted and bubbly.

9. Garnish with chopped fresh herbs before serving.
10. Enjoy these flavorful and creative stuffed peppers or mushrooms made with your leftover chicken and potatoes!

Chapter (14) Comfort Food Classics: Chicken and Potato Tray Recipes for Cozy Nights

A. Creamy Chicken Alfredo with Roasted Potatoes
Ingredients:
For the Creamy Chicken Alfredo:

- Leftover cooked chicken from the tray, shredded or diced
- 8 oz fettuccine pasta
- 2 tablespoons butter
- 2 cloves garlic, minced
- 1 cup heavy cream
- 1 cup grated Parmesan cheese
- Salt and pepper to taste
- Chopped fresh parsley for garnish

For the Roasted Potatoes:

- Leftover roasted potatoes from the tray
- Olive oil
- Salt and pepper to taste
- Dried herbs (optional)

Instructions:

1. Preheat your oven to 375°F (190°C).
2. Cook the fettuccine pasta according to the package instructions until al dente. Drain and set aside.
3. In a large skillet, melt butter over medium heat. Add minced garlic and cook until fragrant, about 1 minute.
4. Pour in heavy cream and bring to a simmer. Cook for 2-3 minutes, stirring constantly.

5. Gradually stir in grated Parmesan cheese until the sauce is smooth and creamy.
6. Add the leftover cooked chicken to the skillet and stir until heated through. Season with salt and pepper to taste.
7. Toss the cooked fettuccine pasta in the creamy Alfredo sauce until well coated.
8. Transfer the chicken Alfredo pasta to a baking dish.
9. In a separate baking dish, arrange the leftover roasted potatoes. Drizzle with olive oil and season with salt, pepper, and dried herbs if desired.
10. Place both the chicken Alfredo pasta and the roasted potatoes in the preheated oven. Bake for 15-20 minutes, or until heated through.
11. Garnish the chicken Alfredo pasta with chopped fresh parsley before serving.
12. Serve the creamy chicken Alfredo with roasted potatoes hot and enjoy this comforting classic!

B. Chicken Pot Pie Casserole with Potato Topping
Ingredients:

- Leftover cooked chicken from the tray, shredded or diced
- Leftover roasted potatoes from the tray, mashed
- 1 onion, diced
- 2 carrots, diced
- 2 celery stalks, diced
- 2 cloves garlic, minced
- 2 tablespoons butter
- 2 tablespoons all-purpose flour
- 1 cup chicken broth
- 1 cup milk
- Salt and pepper to taste
- 1 cup frozen peas

- Chopped fresh parsley for garnish

Instructions:

1. Preheat your oven to 375°F (190°C).
2. In a large skillet, melt butter over medium heat. Add diced onion, carrots, and celery, and sauté until softened, about 5 minutes.
3. Add minced garlic to the skillet and cook for another minute until fragrant.
4. Stir in all-purpose flour and cook for 1-2 minutes to form a roux.
5. Gradually whisk in chicken broth and milk until smooth. Cook until the mixture thickens, stirring constantly.
6. Add the leftover cooked chicken and frozen peas to the skillet. Season with salt and pepper to taste. Stir until well combined.
7. Transfer the chicken and vegetable mixture to a baking dish.
8. Spread the leftover mashed potatoes over the top of the chicken mixture in the baking dish, creating an even layer.
9. Place the baking dish in the preheated oven and bake for 25-30 minutes, or until the filling is bubbly and the potato topping is golden brown.
10. Garnish with chopped fresh parsley before serving.
11. Serve the chicken pot pie casserole hot and enjoy this comforting and hearty dish!

C. Chicken and Potato Tray Shepherd's Pie
Ingredients:

- Leftover cooked chicken from the tray, shredded or diced
- Leftover roasted potatoes from the tray, mashed
- 1 onion, diced
- 2 carrots, diced

- 2 celery stalks, diced
- 2 cloves garlic, minced
- 2 tablespoons tomato paste
- 1 cup chicken broth
- 1 cup frozen peas
- Salt and pepper to taste
- Chopped fresh parsley for garnish

Instructions:

1. Preheat your oven to 375°F (190°C).
2. In a large skillet, heat a bit of oil over medium heat. Add diced onion, carrots, and celery, and sauté until softened, about 5 minutes.
3. Add minced garlic to the skillet and cook for another minute until fragrant.
4. Stir in tomato paste and cook for 1-2 minutes.
5. Add the leftover cooked chicken, chicken broth, and frozen peas to the skillet. Season with salt and pepper to taste. Stir until well combined.
6. Transfer the chicken and vegetable mixture to a baking dish.
7. Spread the leftover mashed potatoes over the top of the chicken mixture in the baking dish, creating an even layer.
8. Place the baking dish in the preheated oven and bake for 25-30 minutes, or until the filling is bubbly and the potato topping is golden brown.
9. Garnish with chopped fresh parsley before serving.
10. Serve the chicken and potato tray Shepherd's pie hot and enjoy this classic comfort food!

D. Chicken and Potato Tray Mac and Cheese Bake
Ingredients:

- Leftover cooked chicken from the tray, shredded or diced
- Leftover roasted potatoes from the tray, diced
- 8 oz elbow macaroni
- 2 cups shredded cheddar cheese
- 2 tablespoons butter
- 2 tablespoons all-purpose flour
- 2 cups milk
- Salt and pepper to taste
- 1/2 cup breadcrumbs
- Chopped fresh parsley for garnish

Instructions:

1. Preheat your oven to 375°F (190°C).
2. Cook the elbow macaroni according to the package instructions until al dente. Drain and set aside.
3. In a large saucepan, melt butter over medium heat. Stir in all-purpose flour and cook for 1-2 minutes to form a roux.
4. Gradually whisk in milk until smooth. Cook until the mixture thickens, stirring constantly.
5. Stir in shredded cheddar cheese until melted and smooth. Season with salt and pepper to taste.
6. Add the leftover cooked chicken and diced roasted potatoes to the cheese sauce. Stir until well combined.
7. Add the cooked elbow macaroni to the cheese sauce mixture and stir until everything is evenly coated.
8. Transfer the mac and cheese mixture to a baking dish.
9. Sprinkle breadcrumbs over the top of the mac and cheese in the baking dish.
10. Place the baking dish in the preheated oven and bake for 20-25 minutes, or until the breadcrumbs are golden brown and the mac and cheese is bubbly.
11. Garnish with chopped fresh parsley before serving.

12. Serve the chicken and potato tray mac and cheese bake hot and enjoy this ultimate comfort food!

Chapter (15) Summer Sensations: Refreshing Chicken and Potato Tray Dishes

A. Grilled Lemon-Herb Chicken with Potato Salad
Grilled Lemon-Herb Chicken Ingredients:

- 4 boneless, skinless chicken breasts
- Zest and juice of 1 lemon
- 2 tablespoons olive oil
- 2 cloves garlic, minced
- 1 teaspoon dried thyme
- 1 teaspoon dried rosemary
- Salt and pepper to taste
- Fresh parsley for garnish

Potato Salad Ingredients:

- Leftover roasted potatoes from the tray, diced
- 1/4 cup mayonnaise
- 1 tablespoon Dijon mustard
- 1 tablespoon apple cider vinegar
- 2 green onions, thinly sliced
- Salt and pepper to taste

Instructions:

1. In a bowl, whisk together lemon zest, lemon juice, olive oil, minced garlic, dried thyme, dried rosemary, salt, and pepper. Add the chicken breasts to the marinade, ensuring they are well coated. Cover and refrigerate for at least 30 minutes.
2. Preheat your grill to medium-high heat. Remove the chicken breasts from the marinade and grill for 6-8 minutes per side, or

until cooked through and no longer pink in the center. Remove from the grill and let them rest for a few minutes before slicing.

3. In a large bowl, combine the diced roasted potatoes, mayonnaise, Dijon mustard, apple cider vinegar, sliced green onions, salt, and pepper. Mix until well combined.

4. Serve the grilled lemon-herb chicken with the potato salad, garnished with fresh parsley.

B. Chicken and Potato Tray with Watermelon and Feta Salad
Ingredients:

- Leftover cooked chicken from the tray, sliced or diced
- Leftover roasted potatoes from the tray
- 4 cups cubed watermelon
- 1/2 cup crumbled feta cheese
- 1/4 cup fresh mint leaves, chopped
- 2 tablespoons balsamic glaze
- Salt and pepper to taste

Instructions:

1. Arrange the leftover cooked chicken and roasted potatoes on a serving platter.

2. In a large bowl, combine the cubed watermelon, crumbled feta cheese, and chopped fresh mint leaves. Season with salt and pepper to taste and toss gently to combine.

3. Serve the chicken and potato tray alongside the watermelon and feta salad. Drizzle with balsamic glaze just before serving.

C. BBQ Chicken and Potato Tray with Grilled Corn on the Cob
Ingredients:

- Leftover cooked chicken from the tray, shredded or sliced
- Leftover roasted potatoes from the tray
- 4 ears of corn, husked
- BBQ sauce of your choice
- Salt and pepper to taste
- Fresh cilantro for garnish

Instructions:

1. Preheat your grill to medium-high heat.
2. Brush the corn on the cob with olive oil and season with salt and pepper.
3. Grill the corn for about 10-12 minutes, turning occasionally, until tender and lightly charred.
4. In a bowl, toss the leftover cooked chicken and roasted potatoes with BBQ sauce until well coated.
5. Arrange the BBQ chicken and potato mixture on a serving platter.
6. Serve the BBQ chicken and potato tray with grilled corn on the cob. Garnish with fresh cilantro.

D. Chicken and Potato Tray Kabobs with Pineapple and Bell Peppers
Ingredients:

- Leftover cooked chicken from the tray, cubed
- Leftover roasted potatoes from the tray
- 1 cup pineapple chunks
- 1 red bell pepper, cut into chunks
- 1 green bell pepper, cut into chunks
- Olive oil for brushing
- Salt and pepper to taste
- Wooden or metal skewers

Instructions:

1. Preheat your grill to medium-high heat.
2. Thread the leftover cooked chicken, roasted potatoes, pineapple chunks, and bell pepper chunks onto skewers, alternating the ingredients.
3. Brush the kabobs with olive oil and season with salt and pepper.
4. Grill the kabobs for 8-10 minutes, turning occasionally, until the chicken is heated through and the vegetables are tender and lightly charred.
5. Serve the chicken and potato tray kabobs hot off the grill.

❖ Conclusion and Final Thoughts

A. Recap of Key Points and Recipes:

Throughout this collection of chicken and potato tray recipes, we've explored a wide range of culinary possibilities, from classic comfort foods to exotic international flavors. We've learned how versatile chicken and potatoes can be when combined in a tray and cooked together, resulting in delicious and satisfying meals for any occasion.

Some of the standout recipes included traditional favorites like Roasted Chicken and Potato Tray, Lemon Herb Chicken with Garlic Roasted Potatoes, and Chicken Parmesan with Potato Wedges. We also ventured into creative twists with dishes like Thai Coconut Curry Chicken with Roasted Potatoes and Mediterranean Chicken and Potato Bake with Olives and Feta.

Whether you're seeking healthy options, low-carb alternatives, or hearty soups and stews, there's something for everyone in this diverse collection. From weeknight dinners to holiday feasts, these recipes offer convenient solutions without sacrificing flavor.

B. Encouragement for Experimentation and Personalization:

As you embark on your culinary journey, I encourage you to experiment with these recipes and make them your own. Feel free to adjust ingredients, seasonings, and cooking techniques to suit your taste preferences and dietary needs. Don't be afraid to get creative and add your own unique twist to each dish.

Remember that cooking is not only about following recipes but also about expressing your creativity and passion for food. Whether you're a seasoned chef or a novice cook, embrace the joy of cooking and enjoy the process of creating delicious meals for yourself and your loved ones.

C. Suggestions for Further Learning and Exploration in the Kitchen:

If you're eager to expand your culinary repertoire further, consider exploring new ingredients, cuisines, and cooking methods. Here are a few suggestions to enhance your culinary skills and knowledge:

1. Explore New Cuisines: Try cooking dishes from different cultures and regions around the world. Experiment with spices, herbs, and ingredients that are characteristic of various cuisines, such as Thai, Indian, Mexican, or Italian.

2. Learn Basic Cooking Techniques: Mastering fundamental cooking techniques like sautéing, roasting, braising, and grilling will empower you to create a wide variety of dishes with confidence and skill.

3. Attend Cooking Classes or Workshops: Take advantage of cooking classes or workshops offered in your community or online. These opportunities provide hands-on experience and expert guidance to help you improve your culinary abilities.

4. Experiment with Seasonal Ingredients: Embrace seasonal produce and ingredients to inspire your cooking. Visit local farmers' markets or join a community-supported agriculture (CSA) program to discover fresh and seasonal ingredients for your recipes.

5. Document Your Culinary Adventures: Keep a journal or digital record of your culinary experiments, including recipes you've tried, modifications you've made, and dishes you've enjoyed. This will serve as a valuable resource and inspiration for future cooking endeavors.

Remember that cooking is a journey of discovery and growth. Embrace the process, savor the flavors, and enjoy the satisfaction of creating delicious meals to share with others.

Happy cooking!